The Kinsey Corruption

An Exposé on the Most Influential "Scientist" of Our Time

Susan Brinkmann

Based on the book,
Kinsey: Crimes and Consequences
by Dr. Judith Reisman

ASCENSION
PRESS

S *THE CATHOLIC*
TANDARD & TIMES

Published by
Ascension Press
P.O. Box 1990
West Chester, PA 19380
www.ascensionpress.com

To order additional copies, please call 1-888-488-6789 or visit the Catholic Outreach website www.CatholicOutreach.com

Printed in the United States of America

ISBN 1-932645-71-2

TABLE OF CONTENTS

Foreword

I make my living doing something I wish didn't have to be done. I travel around the world exposing the lies of the sexual revolution and proclaiming a message of sexual healing, of sexual *salvation*. Heaven knows we are in need of some good news when it comes to sex. The spiritual, psychological, and physical wounds ushered in by so-called sexual "liberation" go deep—very deep. The good news is that sexual healing and restoration are possible in Christ.

If you want to understand the sexual revolution and the moral decline of America over the last half-century, you simply cannot overlook Alfred Kinsey. Summarizing the important work of Dr. Judith Reisman, award-winning journalist Susan Brinkmann provides the reader with a glimpse into the disturbing world of Kinsey's sex research. Based on faulty methodology, flawed data, and sexual "experiments" criminally imposed on adults, adolescents, children, and even infants—Kinsey's warped view of sex continues to impact nearly every facet of our culture. It has seeped into our marriages, our families, our schools, our hospitals, our laws, our politics—and even our churches.

For a time I myself embraced some of the distortions Kinsey and his heedless followers promoted as "normal." But if promiscuous sex was the norm—the way it "should be"—and all restraint a matter of antiquated religious taboos, why, then, did my sexual "liberties" cause me and others such pain? I began asking myself this question during my college years as I pondered the wounded hearts, diseased bodies, and shattered lives that were—

1

thanks in no small part to Kinsey—a "normal" part of college dorm life.

Brinkmann reports that Kinsey was raised in a strict Christian home where dancing, smoking, drinking, and dating were forbidden. I wonder if this might not provide a clue to deciphering the man and his motivations. A religion of mere prohibitions never corresponds to the mystery of the human person and the longings of the human heart. Yet many people consider Christianity—especially when it comes to sexual morality—nothing but a long list of oppressive prohibitions. What a tragic impoverishment of the good news proclaimed by Jesus Christ!

Christ did not die on a cross and rise from the dead to impose a long list of oppressive rules on us. He died on a cross and rose from the dead to set us free from the rules—not free to break them but free to *fulfill* them (see Matthew 5:17, Romans 7, Galatians 5). Christ's redeeming love liberates us from lustful, utilitarian attitudes so that we can be the men and women we are created to be; so that we can love as we are called to love. True freedom, then, is not liberation from the *external* "constraint" that calls us to good, as Kinsey imagined. True freedom is liberation from the *internal* constraint that hinders our choice of the good.

Deep in the heart we experience a war between good and evil, between love and all that is opposed to love. No one is freer than he who, in the midst of this battle, sees what is true, good, and beautiful, desires it with all his heart, and freely chooses it. Absent this "freedom for which Christ has set us free" (Galatians 5:1), religion quickly becomes an imposition of rules. Imposing rules on people, even sound rules (and all the more so arbitrary ones), inspires rebellion.

Kinsey came of age in an era in which the sight of a woman's ankle could cause scandal. A prudish and rigorist climate will eventually propel a person (and the culture) to the other extreme. I say this in no way to justify Kinsey's horrors—only, perhaps, to understand them a little better, and to point out that returning to puritan silence on matters of sex is *not* the solution to the revolution Kinsey inspired. What is needed is a new language that demonstrates the *beauty* of God's plan for sex and the *joy* of living it. Somehow we need to demonstrate to the modern world that the Christian sexual ethic—far from the cramped, prudish list of prohibitions it is usually assumed to be—is actually a liberating message of salvation that corresponds perfectly with the deepest yearnings of the heart for love, intimacy, touch, and affirmation.

God grants the Church what she needs when she needs it. In the past twenty years in America and throughout the world, a new group of scientists, writers, philosophers, theologians, pro-life apologists, and chastity speakers have arisen with an engaging and persuasive defense of Judeo-Christian morality. A large number of these new defenders of man's true dignity, myself included, draw their inspiration from the life and teaching of Pope John Paul II. This Polish philosopher and theologian has made an extraordinary contribution to human thought which the Church and the world will be unfolding for centuries.

Many scholars consider his extended teaching on sexual love and the human person—known as the "theology of the body"—the antidote to the distortions promoted by Kinsey. Catholic theologian George Weigel calls John Paul II's theology of the body "one of the boldest reconfigurations of Catholic theology in centuries...a kind of *theological time-bomb* set to go off with dramatic consequences...perhaps in the twenty-first century" (*Witness to Hope*, pp. 336, 343).

Building on the insights of the greatest saints and mystics, John Paul II teaches us that God created sexual love to be an "icon" of his own divine love—an earthly sign that points us to a heavenly mystery (see Ephesians 5:31-32). When we lose sight of God's loving plan for humanity, however, the icon (the union of the sexes) quickly degenerates into an idol. We come, as St. Paul observed, to worship the creature rather than the Creator. God, in turn, surrenders us to our own disordered passions, to a base mind, and to improper conduct. Men and women give up natural relations and pursue all manner of sexual distortions (see Romans 1: 25-28).

Welcome to the world according to Kinsey. In such a world, man's most base, fallen inclinations are considered "normal." In such a world, sexual pleasure—attained in whatever manner desired—is considered man's right and ultimate fulfillment. In such a world, the "icon" of sexual union has become an idol, an object worshiped in God's place.

Despite the horrors, an important element of truth remains in Kinsey's idolatrous obsession with sex. Behind every false god we discover our desire for the true God gone awry. The sexual confusion so prevalent in our world and in our own hearts is simply the human desire for heaven gone berserk. Untwist Kinsey's distortions and we discover the astounding glory of sex in the divine plan: God created us male and female and calls us to unite in a fruitful, ecstatic union in order to prepare us for eternal love, eternal union, eternal bliss. Sex, then, is only what it is meant to be to the degree that it enables us to enter into the love with which God has loved us from eternity.

Every man and woman desires this love yet every man and woman has fallen short of it. God sent his Son into the world not to condemn us for our failures to love. He sent his Son into the world to save us, to restore in us our true humanity and to fulfill the deepest yearnings of our hearts. This is the "good news" we have to proclaim to a world fast committing sexual suicide.

Perhaps if Kinsey had been raised with this liberating vision rather than with a long list of prohibitions, the world would be a different place. It still can be if we take up this vision and share it with the world in a new evangelization.

—Christopher West
Author of *Good News About Sex and Marriage*
September 20, 2004

Author's note: Those wishing more detailed information on the sources quoted throughout this book should consult Dr. Judith Reisman's work *Kinsey: Crimes and Consequences* (Crestwood, KY: The Institute for Media Education, 1998, 2000), in which all quotations and references are thoroughly documented.

Caution: Some of the subject matter discussed herein is of a sensitive nature and is not appropriate for younger children.

KINSEY: A QUESTION-AND-ANSWER OVERVIEW

Editor's Note: To raise your awareness about the devastating impact of Alfred C. Kinsey and his work, we offer you the following twenty questions which summarize some key aspects of the man and his "research." The answers to these questions have been adapted from the chapters which follow.

1) Who was Alfred Kinsey and why is he a controversial figure?

Alfred Kinsey become a household name in the late 1940s and early 1950s due to the notoriety surrounding the publication of his books *Sexual Behavior in the Human Male* (1948) and *Sexual Behavior in the Human Female* (1952), written while he was a professor at Indiana University. These books were based on questionable research conducted by Kinsey in the area of human sexuality, and they made claims that sent shock waves through our culture and scandalized many. Despite its seriously-flawed methodology, Kisney's research was accepted as scientific fact by many. It led directly to the establishment of modern sex education programs, and paved the way for society to accept behaviors that were previously considered morally illicit, even depraved.

2) What can you tell me about the new movie based on Kinsey's life?

Produced by renowned director Francis Ford Coppola (*The Godfather, Apocalypse Now*), the film *Kinsey* is a major

Hollywood production starring "A-list" actor Liam Neeson (*Shindler's List, Rob Roy, Excalibur*) in the title role. Other prominent cast members include Oscar-nominated Laura Linney (*The Truman Show, Mystic River, You Can Count on Me*), Chris O'Donnell (*Batman, Scent of a Woman, Fried Green Tomatoes*), Oscar-winner Timothy Hutton (*Ordinary People, Taps*), John Lithgow (*Shrek, Pelican Brief, Third Rock from the Sun*), Oliver Platt (*A Time to Kill, Bulworth, The West Wing*), and Tim Curry (*Charlie's Angels, Might Ducks, Home Alone II*).

According to several Christian movie reviewers, the film lionizes Kinsey and sends the message that people who advocate traditional morality are sexually repressed. It also glosses over many of Kinsey's most inexcusable and abhorrent actions, including the use of filmed sexual abuse of children in his research.

3) What do we know about Kinsey's life?

Alfred Charles Kinsey was born in Hoboken, New Jersey on June 23, 1894. He was raised in a strict Methodist home where dancing, tobacco, alcohol, and dating were forbidden. He would eventually sever all ties with his parents—and their religion—and lived the rest of his life as an avowed atheist.

He attended Bowdoin College as a zoology major with a primary interest in insects, graduating in 1916 and electing to continue these studies at Harvard's Bussy Institution. His beliefs found ample nourishment at Harvard, where Darwinism, the "New Biology," and atheism were enjoying immense popularity on campus.

Although early Kinsey biographers like Cornelia Christenson portray Kinsey as shy and disinterested in sex, later biographers discovered a much different picture from Kinsey's personal correspondence, namely that he was homosexual who had a particular interest in young boys. Kinsey's interest in young boys continued after college and into his professorship at Indiana University.

In 1938, his career as a "sex researcher" began when the Association of Women Students at Indiana University asked him to create a "marriage course" on human sexuality for students who were either engaged or married. Indiana University still insists Kinsey was chosen because he was a well-respected professor of zoology, a "disinterested scientist, a person with no ax to grind..." despite substantial evidence to the contrary.

4) Did Kinsey keep his secret life hidden from the public?

Yes, by necessity. Commenting on Kinsey's outrageous conduct, James H. Jones, in his biography *Alfred C. Kinsey: A Public and Private Life,* remarked that "Professors did not engage in that sort of behavior with their graduate students, yet Kinsey seemed totally oblivious to sexual taboos...as though he was determined to flaunt them... Kinsey had become a sexual rebel...manipulative and aggressive, a man who abused his professional authority and betrayed his trust as a teacher. Only a compulsive man would have taken such risks."

This is especially true since the American public of the 1940s and '50s would never have sanctioned the work of a scientist who conducted himself in this manner. Jones writes: "Any disclosure of any feature of this private life...would have been catastrophic for his career. For Kinsey, life in the closet came complete with a wife and children...a public image that he preserved at all costs."

He went to great lengths to burnish his image. After the death of one of his closest friends, Ralph Voris, he and his wife Clara drove all the way from Indiana to Ohio to secretly remove correspondence from Voris' office that revealed incriminating details about Kinsey's homosexuality, such as a collection of "gorgeous" male homosexual photographs that he frequently bragged about to Voris.

5) What were Kinsey's "sex histories"?

Kinsey created a questionnaire of 350 questions which would become the basis for his infamous "interviews" or "sex histories," and the data acquired would be used in his two major publications, *Sexual Behavior in the Human Male* and *Sexual Behavior in the Human Female.*

The questions asked in this questionnaire were so intimate they would be considered an invasion of privacy by today's standards. For instance, interviewees were asked when—not if—they had participated in any violent sadistic sex acts and experimented with members of the same sex, children, and animals.

The collection of these histories was of critical importance to Kinsey's "research," and he went to great lengths to obtain them—not an easy feat during the 1940s. He was prone to badgering and even bullying people to get them. This included students, university professors, and administrators, whose histories contained details about adulterous and homosexual activity unknown to anyone but Kinsey—details which gave Kinsey considerable leverage over the victims of his "research."

6) Is it true that Kinsey, as part of his "research," forced his co-workers to appear in sexually-explicit films?

Yes. Sex histories were not the only lurid requirement of anyone hired by Kinsey. His assistants, Wardell Pomeroy, Clyde Martin, and Paul Gebhard, were also required to be filmed in intimate sexual situations. Filming took place on the Indiana campus or in the attic of the Kinsey home by professional cinematographers Bill Dahlenback and Clarence Tripp.

This requirement was also imposed upon family members of the staff. The wife of one staff member describes the "sickening pressure" put on her to agree to have sex on film. Dr. Judith Reisman cites a film in the Kinsey library that shows a woman who, despite her obvious distress, was bullied into a sexual performance by her husband.

7) Why weren't Kinsey's works criticized by credentialed experts?

They were. Some of the world's most prestigious scientists complained about Kinsey's unscientific methodology. For instance, the questionnaire Kinsey used to collect his data asked questions of such an intimate and private nature that the people who would answer it were primarily deviants and incarcerated sex offenders. The distinguished British medical journal *The Lancet* warned the public that Kinsey had "questioned an unrepresentative proportion of prison inmates and sex offenders in a survey of normal sexual behavior."

This methodology may also have contributed to a lack of professional expertise among those chosen to work on

Kinsey's team. For instance, Clyde Martin, a key Kinsey aide and co-author, had no background or training in statistics, and yet he was charged with all statistical analysis of data. Even complaints from Kinsey's main financier, the Rockefeller Foundation, about the absence of a professional statistician on the staff could not persuade Kinsey to fix this critical problem. Dr. Reisman suspects he was unable to find a credible statistician who possessed the degree of sexual deviancy and anti-religious bias he required. Other leading scientists have offered similar critiques as well.

8) Is it true that Kinsey used known child molesters as "research assistants" for "experiments" with children?

Yes. Not all of Kinsey's horrendous "research" was done at Indiana University. Most was actually conducted "in the field." Reisman cites Kinsey's first book, which claims that additional "sources of data on pre-adolescent boys came from 'the histories of adult males who had sexual contacts with younger boys, and who, with their adult backgrounds were able to recognize and interpret the boys' experiences. Some of these adults were technically-trained persons who have kept diaries or other records...'"

In an audiotaped interview, Kinsey assistant Paul Gebhard responded: "Most of it was done by one individual, a man with scientific training, and not a known scientist."

Reisman discovered that the "man with scientific training" who conducted the experiments on children was referred to as "Mr. X" and, for many years, his identity Mr. X was kept secret. But he was finally discovered to be Rex King, a serial child rapist responsible for the rapes of more than 800 children. Some of these "scientific research" rapes were rendered to Kinsey in graphic detail.

10) Was this fact ever confirmed or denied by Kinsey or the Kinsey Institute?

In an unusually candid 1992 telephone interview with Dr. J. Gordon Muir, Judith Reisman's editor, Paul Gebhard confirmed that some of the men interviewed included child molesters who were easily obtained from prisons and pedophile organizations around the world. He explained that the Kinsey Institute would ask the pedophile how many children they had "done it with," what were the ages of the children, and if the pedophile thought the child had come to climax. He also admitted he was aware of the child abuse inherent in Kinsey's research.

Jonathon Gathorne-Hardy, a Kinsey biographer, received permission from current Kinsey Institute director, John Bancroft, to read and copy Kinsey's pedophile team reports. These and other findings were recorded in a 1998 British documentary titled, *Secret History: Kinsey's Pedophiles*. England's BBC Radio Times called the film "a deeply unsettling documentary...making a strong case that Kinsey cultivated [pedophiles whose crimes] he presented as scientific data." The documentary is now in the hands of people who are deeply concerned about the effects of Kinsey's work and intend to broadcast the documentary. Visit the www.KinseyOutreach.com website regularly to get updates on the broadcasting of this documentary.

11) Is it true that Kinsey also got some of his "research" data from a former Nazi?

Yes, it is true. Dr. Reisman writes that the producers of *Secret History* located another Kinsey accomplice in Berlin: Dr. Fritz Von Balluseck, a notorious Nazi pedophile who contributed his child abuse data during the twenty-year period of 1936 to 1956 to Kinsey's research data base.

Von Balluseck was tried in Berlin in 1957 for the murder of ten-year-old Loiselotte Has. He was described as "the most important pedophile in the criminal history of Berlin," who had sexually violated hundreds of children over the course of thirty years. Von Balluseck sent details of his experiences to Kinsey on a regular basis. Letters from Kinsey to Von Ballusek encouraging the Nazi to continue his "research" were found and reviewed by the presiding judge, Dr. Henrich Berger. Berger repeatedly expressed his outrage at Kinsey for not turning Von Ballusek in to the authorities. Not only did Von Balluseck sexually assault his own daughter, the German press reported that he also raped the eleven-year-old son of a vicar and forced the boy to write down the acts for Kinsey.

12) What effect did Kinsey's works have on American law?

Kinsey's work seriously affected the development of the Model Penal Code (MPC). In *A History of American Law*, Lawrence Friedman writes that the MPC was originally intended "for the persuasion of judges rather than enactment into law," but eventually, the United States Supreme Court and every law school accepted the new Code as authoritative.

"The Model Penal Code of 1955 is virtually a Kinsey document," said Kinsey biographer, Jonathan Gathorne-Hardy. "At one point, Kinsey is cited six times in twelve pages."

Dr. Reisman writes: "At the very time the American Law Institute's Model Penal Code was being developed, there was a growing public outcry for tightening, not loosening, what we called 'sexual psychopath' laws. But respected magistrate Morris Ploscowe, one of the MPC's principal authors, argued based on Kinsey's findings, that 'when a total clean-up of sex offenders is demanded, it is in effect a proposal to put 95 percent of the male population in jail ...'"

Reisman lists some of Kinsey's misleading data that appeared in Ploscowe's work calling for a change in U.S. law regarding sex: "'These pre-marital, extra-marital, homosexual and animal contacts, we are told, are eventually indulged in by 95 percent of the population in violation of statutory prohibitions. If these conclusions are correct, then it is obvious that our sex crime legislation is completely out of touch with the realities of individual living...'"

In *Sexual Patterns and the Law*, Ploscowe writes: "One of the conclusions of the Kinsey report is that the sex-offender is not a monster...but an individual who is not very different from others in his social group, and that his behavior is similar to theirs. The only difference is that others in the offender's social group have not been apprehended. This recognition that there is nothing very shocking or abnormal in the sex offender's behavior should lead to other changes in sex legislation...In the first place, it should lead to a downward revision of the penalties presently imposed on sex offenders." Think about the affect such logic would have on our court systems.

Ploscowe published his own book in 1951, based on Kinsey's work, which has been used for decades in criminal and civil cases relating to human sexual behavior. His publication was one of four major works published by the academic and legal community supporting Kinsey and calling for a change in the law based on his studies.

13) How could this radical change in American law take place given the skepticism many had toward Kinsey's conclusions?

In *About the Kinsey Report*, published in May, 1948, eleven renowned intellectuals representing major Ivy League universities supported Kinsey's science as a collection of factual, objective data. These academics were "completely sold on the Kinsey myth and declared him to be a conservative and impartial American academic whose only interest was to set the record straight."

But Kinsey's most influential supporter was attorney Morris L. Ernst, a founder of the American Civil Liberties Union (ACLU). He served as a personal representative for President Roosevelt during World War II, was the attorney for Alfred Kinsey, Margaret Sanger (the founder of Planned Parenthood), the Kinsey Institute, the Sexuality Information and Education Council of the U.S. (SIECUS) and Planned Parenthood of America. Ernst had close ties to influential and progressive Supreme Court Justices Brandeis, Brennan, and Frankfurter, and Judge Learned Hand, among others.

Dr. Reisman reports Ernst "advocated the legalization of adultery, obscenity and abortion throughout his career, as well as Kinsey's full panoply of sex law changes." According to Ernst, Kinsey's false data first entered into the stream of law through the MPC tentative draft number four, dealing with sex offenses, on April 25, 1955.

Reisman writes: "Standing on the notion of the alleged right of privacy, the Kinsey legal cadre judged the 52 protective sex crime laws as largely illegitimate. By accepting Kinsey's data, almost all sex acts would be restated as private and not subject to social control."

This resulted in radical changes in American sex law. Reisman writes. "Kinsey would indeed impact the American justice system at large by being cited as the 'scientific expert'...who supposedly proved that sex offenders were 95 percent of America's fathers and beloved male family members. The MPC authors demanded and facilitated a downward revision of sex offender penalties because Kinsey said the law was out of step with reality."

14) What was Kinsey's view of rape?

Kinsey considered rape a crime "easily forgotten" by its victims. He is quoted in a book by Susan Brownmiller, *Against Our Will: Men, Women and Rape,* as saying "the only difference between rape and a good time depends on whether the girl's parents were awake when she finally came home."

Assuming Kinsey to be a real scientist, this kind of "data" about women and rape convinced the authors of the Model Penal Code that the justification for tough rape laws was largely moot. The American Bar Association and the American Law Institute established new regulations defining rape and loosening the penalties.

The consequences of this loosening of the law are not surprising. Of the 324 homicides in New York in 1930, 1935, and 1940 (an average of 108 per year), only seventeen (or six per year) involved the rape of women or children. "FBI data for 1995 shows that New York experienced 4,654 murders in 1995, [and] 3,333 were rape-murders," Reisman writes.

15) How did the effect of Kinsey's research on American law contribute to an increase in child molestation?

On the basis of his criminally-obtained "data," Kinsey claimed that children are sexual from birth. Kinsey claimed his research showed that children were harmed more by hysterical parents than by whatever sexual contact they might have had. This led to the loosening of laws regarding pedophilia as well as incest.

In a book authored by the Kinsey team, *Sex Offenders*, they write: "The horror with which our society views the adult who has sexual contact with young children is lessened when one examines the behavior of other mammals. Sexual activity between adults and immature animals is common and appears to be biologically normal." In other words, human behavior is supposed to emulate animals.

These softening attitudes eventually led to lighter sentencing and to the early release of convicted rapists and pedophiles back into society. Reisman writes: "...Only half of the convicted criminals receive prison sentences. Those who do receive time, serve about half of their sentence prior to parole. And of those paroled, half are recorded as recidivists (breaking parole, or committing new crimes when free)."

16) Today, the institution of marriage seems weaker than ever. How much of this can be traced back to Kinsey?

On page 208 of the Model Penal Code, Kinsey's data on adultery is cited as having found that "in an appreciable number of cases, an experiment in adultery tends to confirm rather than disrupt the marriage."

Reisman writes: "The argument was that legalizing fornication and adultery would have little negative effect on society since, according to Kinsey, fornication and adultery were already common among all socioeconomic groups...Once believed, Kinsey's fornication and adultery data...contributed to the erosion of marriage..."

17) How did Kinsey's "sordid science" contribute to the legalization of abortion?

"The Model Penal Code was cited as a national authority on abortion three times in Justice Blackmun's written opinion in *Roe v. Wade*," Reisman writes. Blackmun cites page 147 of Draft 9 of the Model Penal Code where Dr. Mary Calderone of Planned Parenthood states that Kinsey's "scientific" data proved that "90 to 95 percent of pre-marital pregnancies are aborted."

Of course, we now know that Kinsey's data was collected mostly from among prostitutes and sexually-unconventional women and then passed off as indicative of the general population—and more than 45 million pre-born Americans have already paid for this junk science with their lives.

18) What is the connection between the Kinsey Institute and the pornography industry?

In her research, Dr. Judith Reisman discovered that not only was Kinsey linked with the world of pornography, the Kinsey Institute was actually funded by *Playboy* in the 1960s.

In the 1954 Congressional investigation by Congressman B. Carroll Reece of Tennessee, the Rockefeller Foundation, Kinsey's main financier, came under intense scrutiny. The unscientific character of Kinsey's conclusions led the Foundation's president, Dean Rusk, to terminate financial support of the Institute.

Playboy stepped in to provide the funds that launched Kinsey's false sex data into mainstream America. *Playboy,* the Kinsey Institute, *Penthouse,* and *Hustler* went on to form an unholy alliance with prominent sex institutions in the United States, the same institutions that provide the nation's sex education.

19) What has resulted from the widespread availability of pornography in our society? Can its prevalence be traced back to Kinsey?

The negative influence of these materials is beyond question. As Reisman notes, "That *Playboy* and other producers of 'sexually explicit materials' encourage illegal juvenile sexual activity and copy-cat crimes, including incest and child sex abuse, is documented in my peer-approved U.S. Department of Juvenile Justice report, obtainable via the U.S. Department of Justice website."

Also available on the website is Dr. Reisman's study linking erotica/pornography to the legitimization of child pornography. She writes, "Even now, child pornography can be ordered from *Playboy's* earlier editions and from other mainstream pornographic magazines as well as via the *Playboy Press* productions."

In a study of 36 serial sex murderers interviewed by the FBI, 81 percent admitted using pornography. Of those studied, 87 percent of girl child molesters and 77 percent of boy child molesters admitted to regular use of pornography.

Decriminalizing pornography came about when the U.S. Supreme Court accepted the revolutionary Model Penal Code with its recommendation of drastically reducing the penalties for its 52 major sex crimes according to Kinsey's data.

The new Model Penal Code declared a thing obscene if "considered as a whole, its predominant appeal is to prurient interest...And if it goes substantially beyond customary limits of candor in description ..." According to Kinsey, sexual activities such as sodomy incest, pedophilia, and bestiality are within customary limits, so one is left to wonder what exactly the Model Penal Code restricts.

20) How did Kinsey's work manage to invade our "sex education" programs?

After his death in 1956, long-time Kinsey staff members Wardell Pomeroy, Clyde Martin, and Paul Gebhard remained at the Institute and began to train others in Kinsey's "New Biology." Pomeroy left the Institute in 1968 to become the director of the Institute for the Advanced Study of Human Sexuality (IASHS) in San

Francisco, which offered the most extensive training available in the Kinsey model. Pomeroy, who was also a board member of *Penthouse Forum*, was joined in this venture by other major porn personalities such as *Hustler* magazine contributors Ted McIlvenna and Erwin Haeberle.

The Kinsey Institute launched its own organization, the Sexuality Information and Education Council of the U.S. (SIECUS) in 1964 for the proliferation of this "New Biology." Its early leader was Dr. Mary Calderone, the past medical director of Planned Parenthood. The *Playboy* Foundation made the initial grant to establish SIECUS. Considering its backers, one can hardly wonder how sexually explicit materials are getting into the nation's classrooms.

In 1991, SIECUS issued guidelines for sexuality education that were aimed at institutionalizing Kinseyan sexuality nationwide. Reisman writes, "Building on their virtual sex education monopoly, only Kinsey-trained teachers would be permitted in American schoolrooms (K-12) to develop 'sexuality literacy.'"

Reisman writes, "In the early 1980s, *Time* magazine dared twice to expose SIECUS matriarch Calderone and other key sex educators who claimed 'anything goes' for—and with—children. The April 14, 1980 issue of *Time* cited the SIECUS paper on incest, 'Attacking the Last Taboo,' which claimed that "we are roughly in the same position today regarding incest as we were a hundred years ago..." Concluded *Time*, SIECUS was part of an academic "pro-incest lobby...conducting a campaign to undermine the taboo against incest, and all other sexual inhibitions— the Kinsey model."

INTRODUCTION

Except for those too young to remember, there is not a person in America who hasn't wondered about the rapid decline of morality in this country. In just forty years, we have gone from a country of traditional family values to a nation of widespread promiscuity, cohabitation, and soaring divorce rates. At the same time, crime rates have exploded, particularly sex crimes against women and children. How could things go so wrong so fast?

Many experts answer this question with two words: sex research.

It all began in 1948 with the publication of a book entitled *Sexual Behavior in the Human Male,* written by a man named Alfred C. Kinsey of Indiana University. This book contained what was purported to be startling new revelations about human sexuality, most of which shattered all previous traditional notions about mankind's most intimate behavior. Some of these conclusions were: children are sexual from birth; sexual promiscuity is normal; rape is one of the most "forgettable" crimes against women; the only difference between the average man and the sex offender is that one got caught and the other didn't.

In spite of its controversial content, the book was an enormous success, mostly because of its timing and the well-funded media blitz that surrounded it. Launched during the early days of America's infatuation with science, its author, Kinsey, was presented to the public as an upstanding Midwestern family man who was employed by the prestigious Indiana University. Not until after his death in 1956 did biographers begin to uncover a few cracks in the carefully constructed veneer of respectability that surrounded Alfred C. Kinsey and his work.

According to his own personal correspondence, Kinsey was a homosexual with a marked preference for young boys. He was also an atheist and a confirmed bigot who refused to hire Jews, blacks, Christians, and anyone who embraced traditional moral values. He oversaw the filming of live sex acts at Indiana University and in his home, which were performed by members of his own staff and their families, all of whom were expected to participate whether they wanted to or not.

Even more damaging were revelations about how Kinsey conducted his "research" regarding child sexuality. The determination that "children are sexual from birth" was deducted from "data" he collected from pedophiles who regularly sent him the details of their sordid crimes. A 1998 British documentary, *Secret History: Kinsey's Pedophiles,* documents the case of a notorious German pedophile who was on trial for the rape and murder of a ten-year-old girl when his personal correspondence with Kinsey was uncovered. The film was never shown in the United States.

And for good reason. The American public would never accept this behavior from anyone claiming to be a legitimate scientist.

But that's exactly what Alfred C. Kinsey purported to be, even though the real scientific community raised serious questions about his research at the time of his first publication. Some of the world's most prestigious scientists complained about his unscientific methodology. For instance, the questionnaire Kinsey used to collect his data asked questions of such an intimate and private nature that the only people who would answer it were deviants and incarcerated sex offenders. Even the distinguished British medical journal *The Lancet* warned the public that Kinsey had "questioned an unrepresentative proportion of prison inmates and sex offenders in a survey of normal sexual behavior."

And why was there never a professional statistician on Kinsey's staff even though his deductions were entirely based upon the statistical analysis of data?

But Kinsey's work was being funded by money from the Rockefeller Foundation, which was more than enough to eclipse these complaints and launch a second book. *Sexual Behavior in the Human Female* was published in 1952 and again relied upon a database full of prostitutes and other female sexual non-conformists.

While the scientific community continued to clamor for clarity, Indiana University established the powerful Kinsey Institute and began to disseminate Kinsey's bogus data in what would become a new field of science—sex research. Aligned with *Playboy* and Planned Parenthood, the Kinsey-founded Sexuality Information and Education Council of the United States (SIECUS) would eventually become the number one provider of America's sex-education programs.

In the half-century since Kinsey's death, this bogus behavioral information wove its way into the moral fabric of our nation, from the individual to the family, from the classroom to the courtroom. Meanwhile, a whole new cottage industry grew up around the nation's increasing immorality—the sex industry. Anxious to serve our new needs, pornography, sex education and what is politely called "women's reproductive health"— i.e., abortion, sterilization, and birth control—now rake in billions of dollars a year.

And let's not forget Hollywood, which has pocketed the most from our moral decline and has done more than its share to maintain the momentum of our nation's downward spiral. But the movie they filmed in the spring of 2003 goes beyond the pale. Starring Liam Neeson and scheduled for release in late 2004, it presents the life and work of Alfred C. Kinsey in the most glowing terms. Instead of presenting the facts, it glorifies him as a persecuted hero who found himself trapped in a world of sexual repression.

Thankfully, many experts are sounding the alarm. One of them is Dr. Judith Reisman, an internationally renowned authority on Alfred C. Kinsey's false sex data, who addressed the Catholic Leadership Institute at the Wyndham Hotel in Philadelphia in October, 2002. Her audience listened in stunned disbelief as she presented some of the most pristine scholarship on the subject of bogus sex research and how it has contributed to many of today's social ills.

Sporting credentials as sound as her methodology, Reisman earned a doctorate in mass media effects from Case Western Reserve University and went on to study at Haifa University in Jerusalem until the U.S. Department Justice awarded her a full research professorship at American University. Her work has been used by the FBI, the Joint Chiefs of Staff, the Department of Justice, and in a number of international government hearings on science fraud, child sexual abuse, juvenile delinquency, rape and sex crime, and pornography.

But it should be pointed out that Dr. Reisman's interest in the subject is not confined to mere scholarship. Her daughter, Jennie, was raped at the age of ten by a thirteen-year-old boy who later admitted that he drew his inspiration from his father's "girlie magazines." When Reisman broke the news to her family and friends, too many of them tried to comfort her with the notion that "children are sexual from birth." Where were they getting these ideas?

Her search for an answer led her into a world she never knew existed—the world according to Alfred C. Kinsey. What she found there is meticulously documented in her book, *Kinsey: Crimes and Consequences*. Dr. Reisman authorized journalist Susan Brinkmann to write a series of articles based her book. They were published in a seven-part series in *The Catholic Standard and Times* of the Archdiocese of Philadelphia during the summer of 2003. These articles form the basis of this book.

Chapter One

THE EARLY YEARS

Alfred Charles Kinsey was born in Hoboken, New Jersey on June 23, 1894. Raised in a strict Methodist home, he would eventually sever all ties with his parents—and their religion—and live the rest of his life as an avowed atheist.

He attended Bowdoin College as a zoology major with a primary interest in insects, graduating in 1916 and electing to continue these studies at Harvard's Bussy Institution. His atheistic beliefs found ample nourishment at Harvard where Darwinism and the "New Biology," which denied the existence of God, were enjoying immense popularity on campus.

Although early Kinsey biographers, such as Cornelia Christenson, portray Kinsey as being shy and disinterested in sex, later biographers discovered a much different picture from Kinsey's personal correspondence.

As Dr. Reisman documents in her book, *Kinsey: Crimes and Consequences,* the reason he spent so little time around women was because he preferred his own sex, especially young boys. He joined the Boy Scouts as a scout leader at the late age of seventeen, and in a letter he wrote to a fellow Newark YMCA counselor in 1921, Kinsey brags about the "nature library" he kept in his tent that was used as a rendezvous for boys. This "nature library" consisted of nudist magazines that contained drawings and photographs of nude boys as well as adult men.

Kinsey's interest in young boys continued after college and into his professorship at Indiana University. By then, he had married Clara Bracken McMillen, with whom he had four children, one of whom died in childhood. Clara was not only supportive of Kinsey's sexual deviance, she sometimes participated in the wife-swapping and making of sex films with Kinsey staff members in the attic of their home.

She was also quite tolerant of his long camping trips away from home with young male students. During one of these excursions, Kinsey was actually photographed in the nude in the middle of camp. James H. Jones, the author of the biography, *Alfred C. Kinsey: A Public and Private Life*, quotes a student who described Kinsey's habit of bathing with his students and "...striding about camp naked. You'd see him going to the bathroom...he'd just take a leak right in front of us."

The wife of one of these students was not at all pleased with this behavior and claimed that Kinsey took advantage of the young men in group masturbation sessions.

Commenting about the outrageous conduct in his biography, Jones, who was pro-Kinsey, remarked that "Professors did not engage in that sort of behavior with their graduate students, yet Kinsey seemed totally oblivious to sexual taboos...as though he was determined to flaunt them...Kinsey had become a sexual rebel... manipulative and aggressive, a man who abused his professional authority and betrayed his trust as a teacher. Only a compulsive man would have taken such risks."

This is especially true since the American public of the 1940s and '50s would never have sanctioned the work of a scientist who conducted himself in this manner. Jones writes: "Any disclosure of any feature of this private life...would have been catastrophic for his career. For Kinsey, life in the closet came complete with a wife and children...a public image that he preserved at all costs."

Even in these early days, Kinsey was aware of the necessity of presenting a clean image to the American public. After the death of one of his closest friends, Ralph Voris, he and Clara drove all the way from Indiana to Ohio to secretly remove correspondence from Voris' office that revealed incriminating details about Kinsey's homosexuality, such as a collection of "gorgeous" male homosexual photographs that he frequently bragged about to Voris.

In 1938, his career as a sex researcher officially began when the Association of Women Students at Indiana University asked him to create a "marriage course" on human sexuality for students who were either engaged or married. Indiana University still insists that Kinsey was chosen for the course because he was considered a well-respected professor of zoology, a "disinterested scientist, a person with no ax to grind..." in spite of the substantial evidence to the contrary.

As Dr. Reisman points out, by the time Kinsey arrived in Indiana, he was an avowed atheist who embraced the science of eugenics, which called for the elimination of "lower level" Americans. That he had an "ax to grind" was evident in his life-long refusal to permit blacks, Jews, and committed Christians on his staff.

Beneath the carefully crafted veneer of respectability, Kinsey's marriage course grew in popularity—especially the graphic "biology" sex segments, which caused many complaints among the faculty. Nevertheless, the Board of Trustees approved the course for a second year, along with a list of 350 intimate sexual questions that Kinsey intended to ask students in order to begin compiling data.

These 350 questions would become the basis for his infamous "interviews" or "sex histories," and the data acquired would be used in his two major publications, *Sexual Behavior in the Human Male* and *Sexual Behavior in the Human Female.*

The questions asked in this questionnaire were so intimate they would be considered an invasion of privacy by today's standards. For instance, interviewees were asked when—not if—they had participated in any violent sadistic sex acts and experimented with members of the same sex, children, and animals.

The collection of these histories was of critical importance to Kinsey's "research," and he went to great lengths to obtain them, which wasn't easy during the 1940s. He was increasingly prone to badgering and even bullying people to get them. This did not exclude university professors and administrators, whose histories contained details about adulterous and homosexual activity unknown to anyone but Kinsey.

"Kinsey's possession of such sex secrets amounted to a subtle form of coercion bordering on blackmail," Dr. Reisman writes. The clever use of this control device explains how Kinsey managed to maintain complete support from the university. His close friendship with Herman Wells, the president of the university and a bachelor who lived alone with his mother, also insured the continuation of his work.

The giving of sex histories was not the only lurid requirement of anyone hired by Kinsey. His assistants, who would later become his co-authors, Wardell Pomeroy, Clyde Martin, and Paul Gebhard, were also required to be filmed in intimate sexual situations. The filming took place on the Indiana campus or in the attic of the Kinsey home by professional cinematographers, Bill Dahlenback and Clarence Tripp.

This requirement was also imposed upon family members of the staff, whether they wanted to participate or not. The wife of one staff member describes the "sickening pressure" put on her to agree to have sex on film. Dr. Reisman cites a film in the Kinsey library that shows "a woman who, despite her visible distress, was bullied into a sexual performance by her husband."

In spite of the obvious risks involved, the practice continued because, as Jones wrote in his biography: "Kinsey wanted his staff to understand that as scientists, they are not bound by bourgeois morality."

Alfred Kinsey would exhibit this elitist attitude throughout his career, demanding uncontrolled access to the most intimate aspects of people's lives, claiming it was done in the interest of science.

For this reason, renowned scholar Ashley Montagu believed Kinsey suffered from "scientomania," a condition where the scientist loses control of his desire to know and produces a scientific character that is out of balance. The influence of such characters in the field of science are, in Montagu's opinion, "too frightening to contemplate."

Chapter Two

METHODOLOGICAL NONSENSE

We have already discussed in the previous chapter the high degree of sexual nonconformity required of Kinsey staff members. In *Kinsey: Crimes and Consequences*, Dr. Reisman raises the question of whether or not this requirement contributed to a lack of professional expertise among those chosen to work on Kinsey's team.

For instance, Clyde Martin, a key Kinsey aide and co-author, had no background or training in statistics, and yet he was charged with all of the statistical analysis of data for what would become an internationally-known project. Even complaints from Kinsey's main financier, the Rockefeller Foundation, about the absence of a professional statistician on the staff could not persuade Kinsey to fix this critical problem. Reisman suspects that he was unable to find a credible statistician who possessed the degree of sexual deviancy and anti-religious bias that he required.

These troubles only added to Kinsey's larger problem— a sexually explicit and highly offensive questionnaire that few "typical" American men were willing to answer. This paucity of respondents was made worse by World War II, which had called many men into service, leaving men attending colleges and universities as the only other available source. But few of these men would give the kind of intimate sex histories Kinsey wanted.

Therefore Kinsey was compelled to rely upon "volunteers," mostly deviants and a variety of sexual rebels, including incarcerated criminals, streetwalkers, prostitutes, and other miscellaneous riff-raff. In order to make the data appear representative of the "normal" American population, Kinsey was forced to engage in what is known as "category manipulation."

For example, a category labeled "college-level" was substituted for "college" in order to include men who might conceivably go to college. Such a broad category included just about anyone, from juvenile delinquents to the feeble-minded, who might by some gigantic stretch of the imagination end up in a college classroom one day.

In an outrageous example, Kinsey classified 1,400 criminals and sex offenders as "normal" on the grounds that such miscreants were essentially the same as other men—except that these had gotten caught. The "human males" category could then include incarcerated pedophiles, pederasts, homosexual males, boy prostitutes and miscellaneous sexual predators.

Martin, the "statistician," admitted that criminal and abnormal men permeated the sample to such a degree that the only way to clean it up would amount to rewriting the entire book.

Abraham Maslow, a psychologist of global acclaim in the 1940s, and a friend of Kinsey, had already proven that volunteers in a sex study were usually "unconventional" men and women with high rates of unhealthy and disapproved sexual activity. Relying upon these volunteers—even those not counted among prison populations—would produce results that showed a "falsely high percentage of non-virginity, masturbation, promiscuity and homosexuality in the population."

Which is precisely what happened. According to Kinsey's skewed data, 95 percent of the American male population regularly indulged in deviant sexual activities such as extra-marital affairs, homosexuality, pedophilia, etc.

Maslow offered to help Kinsey clean up the "volunteer error" in his work, but once Kinsey realized how this would compromise the outcome of the data and steer it away from the results he wanted, he abruptly terminated his friendship with Maslow.

In spite of these serious problems, Kinsey's first book, *Sexual Behavior in the Human Male*, was published in 1948 amidst an enormously successful media blitz. Kinsey and his team appeared as typical middle-class Americans in publicity photographs, wearing suits and ties and posing with their wives and children whenever possible. Parading the book under the respectable cover of science, coupled with Rockefeller-connected mass media affiliations, the unconventional research of the so-called "All American" Kinsey team seemed acceptable, even state-of-the-art.

But not everyone was fooled. The authentic scientific community proved themselves to be particularly adroit in discovering the methodological nonsense contained in Kinsey's data.

W. Allen Wallis, the distinguished University of Chicago statistician and past president of the American Statistical Association, found serious flaws in Kinsey's work, not least of which was the fact that one-third of the men interviewed were sex offenders.

Even the esteemed British medical journal *The Lancet* concluded that Kinsey "questioned an unrepresentative proportion of prison inmates and sex offenders in a survey of normal sexual behavior."

Dr. Albert Hobbs, a sociologist and author at the University of Pennsylvania accused Kinsey of violating all three precepts necessary for sound scientific method and procedure.

First, the scientist should not have any preconceived hypothesis in order to present only the facts.

"Kinsey actually had a two-pronged hypothesis," Hobbs said. "He vigorously promoted, juggling his figures to do so, a hedonistic, animalistic conception of sexual behavior, while at the same time he consistently denounced all biblical and conventional conceptions of sexual behavior."

Second, Kinsey refused to publish the basic data upon which his conclusions rested. Third, he refused to reveal the questionnaire upon which he based all of his facts.

The rash of scientific criticism caused Kinsey's financier, the Rockefeller Foundation, to again complain about the absence of a professional statistician on Kinsey's staff. Reisman's book cites a letter from the Foundation to Kinsey on May 7, 1951, which said, in part: "Past and present needs remain unsatisfied in the point of statistics. This fault—this admittedly absolutely basic fault—existed in the project in 1942, it has existed ever since, there is no promise whatsoever that it will cease to exist and we do nothing about it."

Clyde Martin continued on as Kinsey's "statistician," even after the Kinsey Institute released a second book containing more of the same sampling errors in 1952— *Sexual Behavior in the Human Female.*

So few "normal" women would talk to Kinsey and his interviewers that the team depicted untold numbers of sexually unconventional women as normal. Kinsey went so far as to classify as "married" any woman who had lived with a man for at least a year, which could conceivably include working prostitutes.

Reisman writes, "By mixing in prostitutes, Kinsey was able to present sexual promiscuity as normal, including perversions such as sex with animals. Although he excluded 934 black women as unrepresentative of the population, he included 31 females who copulated with animals."

Reisman cites Harriet R. Mowrer, a marital-adjustment consultant who warned of the danger of accepting Kinsey's findings at face value: "To accept the Kinsey findings without exacting scrutiny...would be to perpetuate the error...with harmful results to society... There is no assurance that Kinsey's findings are representative and can be extended to the general population."

Her warnings, and many others like hers, went unheeded. Kinsey's methodological nonsense was applied wholesale to the general population at a cost to society that is almost too staggering to consider.

Chapter Three

THE CHILDREN OF TABLE 34

Some of the most vile sets of statistics came from the infamous Table 34, "Examples of Multiple Orgasm in Pre-Adolescent Males," that appeared in Kinsey's first book. This was the research conducted on children under the age of thirteen, which was presented to the world as proof that erotic arousal was possible in children as young as two months.

"Table 34 was truly grotesque," writes Dr. Reisman in *Kinsey: Crimes and Consequences.* "It reported around-the-clock experimental data on infants and young boys. The Kinsey team seemed perfectly at ease when describing the extraordinary data: 'Even the youngest males, as young as two months of age, are capable of such repeated reactions. Typical cases are shown in Table 34. The maximum observed was 26 climaxes in 24 hours (in a four-year-old and a thirteen-year-old)...'"

How was this data collected?

When Reisman asked this question, she received an answer directly from Kinsey team member, Paul Gebhard, who told her that Kinsey's men used "manual and oral techniques" to produce the orgasms.

Prominent pediatricians who reviewed this data confirm that "children, especially the very young, would not willingly submit to such abuse." Dr. Lester Caplan, a Baltimore physician and member of the American Board of Pediatrics, confirmed in a letter to this author that children could not have voluntarily participated..."

Kinsey himself admits that there was no physical evidence of these so-called "orgasms," and based his conclusions on the children's reactions. Reisman writes: "Kinsey's books were meant to convince the public that we are all sexual—from womb to tomb—so he had to prove infants were lustful, even if that meant tying them down and labeling their hysterical weeping as orgasm."

But not all of this horrendous testing was done at Indiana University. The larger portion was actually conducted "in the field." Reisman cites Kinsey's first book, which claims that additional "sources of data on pre-adolescent boys came from 'the histories of adult males who had sexual contacts with younger boys, and who, with their adult backgrounds were able to recognize and interpret the boys' experiences. Some of these adults were technically-trained persons who have kept diaries or other records...'"

Who were these "technically-trained persons?"

In an audio-taped interview, Paul Gebhard responded: "Most of it was done by one individual, a man with scientific training, and not a known scientist. The other cases were done by parents at our suggestion and, let's see, then there were some that were done by nursery school personnel."

Probing deeper, Reisman discovered that the "man with scientific training" who conducted the experiments on children that were recorded in Table 34, was known as "Mr. X." For many years, the identity of Mr. X was kept secret, but was later discovered to be Rex King, the serial child rapist responsible for the rapes of more than 800 children. Some of these rapes were rendered to Kinsey in graphic detail, which he considered to be "scientific research."

Reisman writes: "Indiana University records confirm that Kinsey did not report Mr. X to authorities. Indeed, for over 50 years the entire Indiana University Kinsey

Institute team collaborated in covering up sex crimes perpetrated against children involved in its research."

In an unusually candid telephone interview on November 2, 1992, with Reisman's editor, J. Gordon Muir, M.D., Paul Gebhard confirmed that some of the men on Kinsey's child sexuality team included child molesters who were easily obtained from prisons and pedophile organizations around the world. He explained that the Kinsey Institute would ask the pedophile how many children they had "done it with," what were the ages of the children, and if the pedophile thought the child had come to climax. He also admitted that he was aware of the child abuse inherent in Kinsey's research.

Jonathon Gathorne-Hardy, a Kinsey biographer, received permission from current Kinsey Institute director, John Bancroft, to read and copy Kinsey's pedophile team reports. These and other findings were recorded in a 1998 British documentary titled, *Secret History: Kinsey's Pedophiles*. England's BBC Radio Times called the film "a deeply unsettling documentary... making a strong case that Kinsey cultivated [pedophiles whose crimes] he presented as scientific data."

The Yorkshire documentary uncovered even more shocking revelations about the so-called "trained persons" who participated in Kinsey's experiments. Reisman writes that the film makers located another Kinsey accomplice in Berlin, Dr. Fritz Von Balluseck, the notorious Nazi pedophile who contributed his child abuse data during the twenty year period of 1936 to 1956 to Kinsey's research data base.

The Von Balluseck case, which involved the murder of ten-year-old Loiselotte Has, was tried in Berlin in 1957 and was widely covered by the German press. Von Balluseck was described as "the most important pedophile in the criminal history of Berlin," who had sexually violated hundreds of children over the course of 30 years.

Apparently, Von Balluseck was sending details of his experiences to Kinsey on a regular basis. Letters from Kinsey to Von Ballusek encouraging the Nazi to continue his "research" were found and reviewed by the presiding judge, Dr. Henrich Berger. Berger repeatedly expressed his outrage at Kinsey for not turning Von Ballusek in to the authorities. Not only did Von Balluseck sexually assault his own daughter, the German press reported that he also raped the eleven-year-old son of a vicar and forced the boy to write down the acts for Kinsey.

The German newspaper, the *National Zeitung* wrote on May 15, 1957: "Today the court has got four diaries and in these diaries with cynicism and passion, he (Von Balluseck) recorded his crimes against 100 children in the smallest detail. He sent the detail of his experiences regularly to the U.S. sex researcher, Kinsey. The latter was very interested and kept up a regular and lively correspondence with Von Ballusek."

Reisman writes: "Despite Alfred Kinsey's shocking role in this explosive case, the U.S. press was uniformly silent about it." Why?

Yale zoologist George A. Baitsell, writing in the *Yale News*, voiced his opinion about how this could have happened: "The abuse inherent in the Kinsey team's methodology has gone largely unheeded by the academic elite, and thousands of world famous doctors, sociologists, sex educators and even ministers...anyone whose careers have largely been built around Kinsey."

Chapter Four

KINSEY'S FLAWED DATA
ENTERS AMERICAN LAW

Between the years of 1948 and 1952, two critical events were taking place in the United States—the introduction of Alfred C. Kinsey's erroneous research into American society, and the development of the Model Penal Code (MPC).

How uncanny that the document containing the nation's sex crime statutes should be in the process of development at the same time as a sex researcher from Indiana was declaring that 95 percent of the American male population participates in deviant sexual activity on a regular basis.

What effect did Kinsey's data actually have on the new Model Penal Code? "The Model Penal Code of 1955 is virtually a Kinsey document," said Kinsey biographer, Jonathan Gathorne-Hardy. "At one point, Kinsey is cited six times in twelve pages." The story goes downhill from here.

In *A History of American Law*, Lawrence Friedman writes that the MPC was originally intended "for the persuasion of judges rather than enactment into law," but eventually, the United States Supreme Court justices and every law school accepted the new Code as authoritative.

In *Kinsey: Crimes and Consequences*, Reisman writes: "At the very time the American Law Institute's Model Penal Code was being developed, there was a growing public outcry for tightening, not loosening, what we called 'sexual psychopath' laws. But respected magistrate Morris Ploscowe, one of the MPC's principal authors, argued based on Kinsey's findings, that 'when a total clean-up of sex offenders is demanded, it is in effect a proposal to put 95 percent of the male population in jail...'"

Reisman lists some of Kinsey's misleading data that appeared in Ploscowe's work calling for a change in U.S. law regarding sex: "'These pre-marital, extra-marital, homosexual and animal contacts, we are told, are eventually indulged in by 95 percent of the population in violation of statutory prohibitions. If these conclusions are correct, then it is obvious that our sex crime legislation is completely out of touch with the realities of individual living...'"

In *Sexual Patterns and the Law*, Ploscowe writes: "One of the conclusions of the Kinsey report is that the sex-offender is not a monster...but an individual who is not very different from others in his social group, and that his behavior is similar to theirs. The only difference is that others in the offender's social group have not been apprehended. This recognition that there is nothing very shocking or abnormal in the sex offender's behavior should lead to other changes in sex legislation...In the first place, it should lead to a downward revision of the penalties presently imposed on sex offenders." Ploscowe published his own tome in 1951, based on Kinsey's statistics, which has been used for decades in criminal and civil cases relating to human sexual behavior. His publication was one of four major works published by the academic and legal community supporting Kinsey and calling for a change in the law based on his studies.

In *About the Kinsey Report*, published in May, 1948, eleven renowned intellectuals representing major Ivy League universities supported Kinsey's science as a collection of factual, objective data. These academics were completely sold on the Kinsey myth and considered him to be "a conservative and impartial American academic whose only interest was to set the record straight."

Probably the most influential supporter of changing the sex laws according to Kinsey's statistics, was attorney Morris L. Ernst, a founding member of the American Civil Liberties Union (ACLU). He served as a personal representative for President Roosevelt during WWII, was the attorney for Alfred Kinsey, Margaret Sanger (the founder of Planned Parenthood), the Kinsey Institute, the Sexuality Information and Education Council of the United States (SIECUS) and Planned Parenthood of America. Ernst had close ties to influential and progressive Supreme Court Justices Brandeis, Brennan, and Frankfurther, and Judge Learned Hand, among others.

Reisman writes that Ernst "advocated the legalization of adultery, obscenity and abortion throughout his career, as well as Kinsey's full panoply of sex law changes." According to Ernst, Kinsey's false data first entered into the stream of law through the MPC tentative draft number four, dealing with sex offenses, on April 25, 1955.

Reisman writes: "Standing on the notion of the alleged right of privacy, the Kinsey legal cadre judged the 52 protective sex crime laws as largely illegitimate. By accepting Kinsey's data, almost all sex acts would be restated as private and not subject to social control."

This resulted in radical changes in American sex law. Reisman writes: "Kinsey would indeed impact the American justice system at large by being cited as the 'scientific expert'...who supposedly proved that sex offenders were 95 percent of America's fathers and beloved male family members. The MPC authors demanded and facilitated a downward revision of sex offender penalties because Kinsey said reality was out of step with the law. This was all based on Kinsey's aberrant groups of criminals, homosexuals, pedophiles, and the like ... The revision lead to the weakening and destruction of 52 sex offender laws targeted for change, and would undermine marriage as the single legitimate source of all coitus."

Reisman goes on to note that: "These distinguished authors hailed from august institutions and were leaders in their professions. They are culpable. They knew, or should have known, that Kinsey was a fraud. (The Rockefeller Foundation knew that his data was totally unreliable.)

"After Kinsey's bogus data entered the stream of law through the MPC draft on sex offenses in 1955, the Kinsey sexuality model became codified as normal in mainstream America. It was taught by many unsuspecting law professors in America's most prestigious law schools."

Reisman evidences this statement by showing over 650 citations to Kinsey in Law Review articles published between 1982 and 2000.

But how could Kinsey get away with all this? There are several reasons, one of which was Kinsey's obsession with concealing his own sexual activities, particularly those concerning sex with children.

Reisman writes: "How sympathetic would legislators have been to Kinsey's pleas (for reduced sex crime penalties) had they known that he concealed the fact that roughly one year earlier his team denied assistance to police regarding a Kinsey aide who was a child sex-murder suspect?"

The public's exaggerated regard for science at the time was a facilitating factor. Reisman writes: "Ironically, after 50 years of saturating America with Kinsey's science and the sexual revolution it incited, the 1999 *Intercollegiate Review* ranked Kinsey's book as the 'third worst book of the century.' It stated: "So mesmerized were Americans by the authority of Science, with a capital *S*, that it took 40 years for anyone to wonder how data is gathered on the sexual responses of children as young as five.'" Added the review, this was "a pervert's attempt to demonstrate that perversion is statistically 'normal.'"

Chapter Five

THE FALLOUT: KINSEY'S DATA, THE LAW, AND AMERICAN SOCIETY

When the fraudulent research of an acknowledged pederast was allowed to influence American law, the fallout was devastating. It caused a deep rending in the moral fiber of the nation.

Soaring Crime Rates
In *Kinsey: Crimes and Consequences,* Dr. Reisman includes actual transcripts of testimony by Alfred Kinsey to the California Legislature where he uses his false data to argue for paroling rapists and even child sex offenders. Unfortunately, he was convincing enough to bring about devastating changes in the law.

For instance, Kinsey considered rape to be a crime "easily forgotten" by its victims. He is quoted in a book by Susan Brownmiller, *Against Our Will: Men, Women and Rape,* as saying "the only difference between rape and a good time depends on whether the girl's parents were awake when she finally came home."

Assuming Kinsey to be a real scientist, this kind of "data" about women and rape convinced the authors of the Model Penal Code that the justification for tough rape laws was largely moot. The American Bar Association and the American Law Institute established new regulations for deciding if a girl was raped.

Reisman writes: "Where the victim is shown to have had a 'racy' past (not exactly defined by the Model Penal Code) for purposes of adjudication she might be labeled a 'prostitute.' Therefore, even when she was the victim of a 'gang' or fraternity 'group' rape, the guilty predator might be cleared of any crime."

The consequences of this loosening of the law against rape are not surprising. The nation is suffering from an epidemic of sexually violent crime, which Reisman lists as: "rape, gang-rape, date rape, rape-mutilation, serial rape-murder, kidnapping-rape, rough sex rape-murder—victimizing the elderly as well as younger boys and girls."

Of the 324 homicides in New York in 1930, 1935, and 1940 (108 per year), only seventeen (or six per year) involved the rape of women or children. "FBI data for 1995 shows that New York experienced 4,654 murders in 1995, [and] 3,333 were rape-murders," Reisman writes.

Another area particularly hard-hit by Kinsey's influence on American law is in the enormous increase in sex crimes committed against children. Spawned by his criminally obtained "data," Kinsey's so-called proof that children are sexual from birth produced the horrifying results listed in Reisman's book: "Current estimates of one in four females (and one in seven boys) have been molested by age eighteen suggests that American children today are experiencing unprecedented rates of sexual abuse."

Kinsey believed his research supported the fact that children were harmed more by their hysterical parents than by whatever sexual contact they might have had. This led to the loosening of laws regarding pedophilia as well as incest.

In a book authored by the Kinsey team, *Sex Offenders*, they write: "The horror with which our society views the adult who has sexual contact with young children is lessened when one examines the behavior of other mammals. Sexual activity between adults and immature animals is common and appears to be biologically normal." In other words, human behavior is supposed to be similar to that of animals.

It should come as no surprise then that by 1973 the American Psychiatric Association (APA) had removed pedophilia—as well as sadism and homosexuality—from its list of "disorders." They stated that the desires to do violence or to have sex with children becomes a disorder only if the pedophile feels guilty or has anxiety about his sexual desires or actions toward the children.

Reisman writes of the APA position on pedophilia and sadism: "The APA published 'study,' in line with the Kinseyan model, has reportedly already been used in the courtroom to erode legal protections that currently penalize child sex offenses—or, as some sexologists euphemistically term it, 'age-discrepant sexual intimacy.'"

These softening attitudes eventually led to lighter sentencing and to the early release of convicted rapists and pedophiles back into society. Reisman writes: "... Only half of the convicted criminals receive prison sentences. Those who do receive time, serve about half of their sentence prior to parole. And of those paroled, half are recorded as recidivists (breaking parole, or committing new crimes when free)."

Perhaps the most dramatic example of the impact on our society of early parole for sex offenders is seen in a 1990 Tacoma, Washington case of a paroled child sex offender who raped and sexually mutilated a seven-year-old boy. Prior to this atrocity, the offender had murdered a fifteen-year-old girl and savagely molested seven other children. He was freed despite these crimes and the authorities' knowledge of his plans to build a "death van" equipped with cages and shackles to be used in the capture and torture of young children. In spite of all this, the man lived next door to an elementary school.

Erosion of Marriage and Family

Another major area where Kinsey data negatively influenced the law and society was in the decriminalization of adultery, cohabitation, and fornication, which lead to an overall weakening in the institution of marriage.

On page 208 of the Model Penal Code, Kinsey's data on adultery is cited as having found that "in an appreciable number of cases, an experiment in adultery tends to confirm rather than disrupt the marriage."

Reisman writes: "The argument was that legalizing fornication and adultery would have little negative effect on society since, according to Kinsey, fornication and adultery were already common among all socioeconomic groups...Once believed, Kinsey's fornication and adultery data...contributed to the erosion of marriage..."

It was an erosion that would eventually bring about no-fault divorce. Originally intended to make it easier for women to escape bad marriages, casual divorce has resulted in making couples less willing to fully commit to their union which, in turn, reduces the likelihood of marital success.

Reisman cites the work of Bryce Christensen, who addressed some of the "appalling societal consequences from no-fault divorce" in *The Family in America* in January, 2000: "The U.S. Census Bureau reported that in 1950, 43 percent of children were at home with Mom while Dad worked full-time. By 1990, only eighteen percent of American children had such a stable home...Thomas B. Marvell calculated in 1989 that the adoption of no-fault statutes had driven up state divorce rates by some twenty to 25 percent. And in a 1999 analysis, a team of statisticians determined that in the 32 states which had enacted no-fault laws by 1974, these laws resulted in substantial number of divorces that would not have occurred otherwise..."

According to Reisman, crime rates and the erosion of the family are only the tip of the iceburg when considering the havoc wreaked upon society by the sex research of a sado-masochistic pedophile. Teen pregnancies, soaring STD and HIV/AIDS rates, rampant cohabitation, and single-parent homes are other areas that have been just as dramatically influenced by the widespread acceptance of Alfred Kinsey's research.

But no member of society has suffered more than our innocent children. Not only for the reasons stated above, but because Alfred Kinsey's distorted studies about women led to one of the most disastrous Supreme Court decisions ever made—*Roe v. Wade.*

"The Model Penal Code was cited as a national authority on abortion three times in Justice Blackmun's written opinion in *Roe v. Wade,*" Reisman writes. Blackmun cites page 147 of Draft 9 of the Model Penal Code where Dr. Mary Calderone of Planned Parenthood states that Kinsey's "scientific" data proved that "90 to 95 percent of pre-marital pregnancies are aborted."

Of course, we now know that Kinsey's data was collected mostly from among prostitutes and sexually unconventional women and then passed off as indicative of the general population.

This kind of sordid science doesn't come without a price—and more than 45 million pre-born Americans have already paid for it with their lives.

Chapter Six

UNHOLY ALLIANCE: ALFRED KINSEY AND THE PORN INDUSTRY

The repudiation of obscenity has long been the hallmark of civil society. In *Kinsey: Crimes and Consequences*, Dr. Reisman points out the centuries-old conclusion that sexually explicit material leads to "copy cat" conduct, which is particularly harmful for children. It results in public disorder and the coarsening of men's attitudes toward women, leading to prostitution and violent sex crimes which, in turn, produce sexual diseases and other factors contributing to early death rates.

In the early days of her research into the harmful effects of pornography on children, Dr. Reisman admits, "I had no notion of the role of Alfred C. Kinsey in pornography or exactly how 'hard'-and-'soft' core pornography related to child sex abuse. I had no idea how bad the problem was or how deeply I would become involved in the attempt to solve it."

What she would discover is still relatively unknown to the American public. Not only was Kinsey linked with the world of pornography, the Kinsey Institute was actually funded by *Playboy* in the 1960s.

It happened after the 1954 Congressional investigation opened by Congressman B. Carroll Reece of Tennessee. The Rockefeller Foundation, Kinsey's main financier, came under intense scrutiny. Kinsey's research was exposed as worthless by credible critics, which caused the Foundation's president and future Secretary of State, Dean Rusk, to terminate financial support of the Institute.

Playboy stepped in to provide the funds that launched Kinsey's false sex data into mainstream America. *Playboy,* the Kinsey Institute, *Penthouse,* and *Hustler* went on to form an unholy alliance with prominent sex institutions in the United States, the same institutions that provide the nation's sex education.

With such close links to the pornography industry, parents need no longer wonder why America's sex education classes and materials are so explicit. In fact, a 1996 report issued by the Kinsey-spawned Sexuality Information and Education Council of the United States (SIECUS) actually urged school teachers to provide "sexually explicit visual, printed or on-line materials" for schoolchildren in order to 'reduce ignorance and confusion' and to help children develop a 'wholesome concept of sexuality.'"

Very few parents in mainstream America would define "wholesome" the same way as Alfred Kinsey and *Playboy* magazine.

The negative influence of these materials is beyond question. Reisman writes, "That *Playboy* and other producers of 'sexually explicit materials' encourage illegal juvenile sexual activity and copy-cat crimes, including incest and child sex abuse, is documented in my peer-approved U.S. Department of Juvenile Justice report, obtainable via the U.S. Department of Justice web site."

Also available on the web site is Dr. Reisman's study linking erotica/pornography to the legitimization of child pornography. She writes, "Even now, child pornography can be ordered from *Playboy's* earlier editions and from other mainstream pornographic magazines as well as via the *Playboy* Press productions."

It is an established fact that child molesters regularly use pornography to seduce their prey, to lower the inhibitions of their young victims and to serve as a kind of "instruction manual."

In a study of 36 serial sex murderers interviewed by the FBI, 81 percent admitted using pornography. Of those studied, 87 percent of girl child molesters and 77 percent of boy child molesters admitted to regular use of pornography.

Decriminalizing pornography came about when the U.S. Supreme Court accepted the revolutionary Model Penal Code with its recommendation of drastically reducing the penalties for its 52 major sex crimes according to Kinsey's data.

Prior to that time, the definition of obscenity according to case law was "anything offensive to chastity or modesty, expressing or presenting to the mind or view something that...decency forbids to be exposed...tending to stir the sex impulses or to lead to sexually impure and lustful thoughts..."

The new Model Penal Code declared a thing obscene if "considered as a whole, its predominant appeal is to prurient interest...And if it goes substantially beyond customary limits of candor in description..." According to Kinsey, sexual activities such as sodomy, incest, pedophilia, and bestiality are within customary limits, so one is left to wonder what exactly the Model Penal Code restricts.

This vague definition allows much in the way of loose interpretation, even in the sex industry itself, where a technique called Sexual Attitude Restructuring (SAR) is used to reform the attitudes of sex instructors.

Reisman describes how students are required to sit through "an orgy of pornographic couplings on film and video...utilized in academia to restructure students' modest sexual attitudes into the bizarre Kinsey alternative..."

George Leonard was one of 60,000 people to go through the Institute for Advanced Study of Human Sexuality (IASHS) by 1982. He described the typical SAR experience of having to endure hours of pornographic films in a kind of "sensory overload" meant to desensitize him to all forms of sex. He sat in the darkness on a Saturday night and watched "images of human beings—and sometimes even animals— engaging in every conceivable sexual act, accompanied by wails, moans, shouts, and the first movement of the Tchaikovsky Violin Concerto..."

"Over a period of several hours, there came a moment when the four images on the wall were of a gay male couple, a straight couple, a lesbian couple, and a bestial group. The subjects were nude...I felt myself becoming disoriented...was she kissing a man or a woman? I couldn't remember which was which. By the end... nothing was shocking...but nothing was sacred either."

Employing the usual Kinsey euphemisms, Dr. Wardell Pomeroy described this process as "designed to desensitize." In other words, brainwash.

"The SAR literally scars the viewers brain as it circumvents, short-circuits, his or her cognition and conscience," Reisman writes. She refers to the findings of Dr. Gary Lynch, a neuroscientist, who compares the damage done by the SAR technique with other high-resonance stimuli, namely, that it produces "a structural change that is in some ways as profound as the structural change one sees in brain damage."

Reisman explains, "Functionally speaking, the SAR (and to a lesser degree, yet with more consistency, today's mass media) breaks down the inhibitions of the healthy brain..."

The (SAR) technique is now widely used to reprogram students in education, medicine, psychology, criminology, and even theology. By reconfiguring their neurochemistry, their human nature, the process has produced "a cadre of educated leaders who are part of the Kinseyan deviance," writes Dr. Reisman.

In the final chapter we will examine how Kinsey-educated sexologists formed themselves into the nation's sex education providers.

Chapter Seven

ALFRED KINSEY AND AMERICAN SEX ED

The many contrived conclusions reached by Alfred C. Kinsey managed to weave themselves into the very fabric of American life. Among others, Kinsey taught that the goal of intercourse should be pleasure, not love, and this paved the way for every conceivable form of noncommittal sexual activity. He also highly recommended sexual activity between adults and children, including incest. All forms of sodomy are natural and healthy, he said, and, with the use of erroneous numbers, tried to prove that homosexuality was more prevalent in our society than heterosexuality.

Even though all of these findings have been thoroughly disproved by credible research and human experience, the Kinsey Institute spawned nearly all of the organizations that provide the nation's sex education curriculums.

In *Kinsey: Crimes and Consequences*, Dr. Reisman writes, "Kinsey's philosophy of early childhood sexual development became the standard for today's graphic sex instruction materials in many, if not most, American public, private and parochial schools, usually camouflaged by such euphemistic captions as sex education, AIDS prevention or awareness, family life, health, hygiene...even abstinence education. Public health data confirm that as Kinsey-based sex education has metastasized, levels of sexual disease and dysfunction have rocketed upward..."

How did Kinsey's sordid science manage to invade our sex ed programs?

It began with the death of Kinsey in August, 1956, shortly after his return from Europe. The official cause of his death was pneumonia brought on by overwork and an enlarged heart. However, other evidence points to complications from what Kinsey called a "pelvic infection," but which was actually diagnosed as orchitis. Orchitis is marked by pain and swelling of the genitals usually caused by gonorrhea, syphilis, filarial disease, or tuberculosis. The condition usually follows some kind of trauma, which, according to Kinsey biographer James H. Jones, Kinsey regularly inflicted upon himself by his compulsive genital self-mutilation and other sado-masochistic behaviors.

Reisman writes, "The sexual revolution faced a potentially serious setback were it widely known that the theoretical father of the movement had died from an advanced stage of sadosexual autoerotic (masturbatory) activity." Kinsey vehemently denied the danger of contracting sexual diseases as a result of the perversions he advocated. For this reason, his death could never be attributed to such causes.

After his death, long-time Kinsey staff members Wardell Pomeroy, Clyde Martin, and Paul Gebhard remained at the Institute and began to train others in Kinsey's "New Biology." Pomeroy left the Institute in 1968 to become the director of the Institute for the Advanced Study of Human Sexuality (IASHS) in San Francisco, which offered the most extensive training available in the Kinsey model. Pomeroy, who was also a board member of *Penthouse Forum*, was joined in this venture by other major porn personalities such as *Hustler* magazine contributors Ted McIlvenna and Erwin Haeberle.

Other accredited sexology degrees in Kinsey's "New Biology" became available from the New York University Health Department's School of Education, under homosexual activist Deryck Calderwood, who would later die of AIDS.

The University of Pennsylvania Department of Health's School of Education also began offering similar training and degrees, directed by homosexual advocate Kenneth George.

These three major academic centers began to train "sexologists" who would eventually design and implement the sex education curricula for all ages of American youth. They did this through the establishment of the Society for the Scientific Study of Sex (SSSS), which was a joint venture by Pomeroy and Gebhard, Calderwood of NYU and Vern Bullough, the editor of *Paidika: The Journal of Pedophilia*. The SSSS established a Commission of Accreditation for the field which granted approval to no one except those who espoused the beliefs of Alfred Kinsey.

The Kinsey Institute launched its own organization, the Sexuality Information and Education Council of the U.S. (SIECUS) in 1964 for the proliferation of this "New Biology." Its early leader was Dr. Mary Calderone, the past medical director of Planned Parenthood. The *Playboy* Foundation made the initial grant to establish SIECUS. Considering its backers, one can hardly wonder how sexually explicit materials are getting into the nation's classrooms.

In 1991, SIECUS issued guidelines for sexuality education that were aimed at institutionalizing Kinseyan sexuality nationwide. Reisman writes, "Building on their virtual sex education monopoly, only Kinsey-trained teachers would be permitted in American schoolrooms (K-12) to develop 'sexuality literacy.'"

SIECUS guidelines suggest that teens should be encouraged to explore "the full range of safe sexual behaviors" so that "we may help to raise a generation of adults that do not equate sex with intercourse..."

In 1992, SIECUS produced a pamphlet called "Talk about Sex," which urged children not to reject the sexually exploitive media that surrounds them, but to use it as a sexual aid.

Reisman writes, "In the early 1980s, *Time* Magazine dared twice to expose SIECUS matriarch Calderone and other key sex educators who claimed 'anything goes' for—and with—children. The April 14, 1980 issue of *Time* cited the SIECUS paper on incest, 'Attacking the Last Taboo,' which claimed that "we are roughly in the same position today regarding incest as we were a hundred years ago..." Concluded *Time*, SIECUS was part of an academic "pro-incest lobby...conducting a campaign to undermine the taboo against incest, and all other sexual inhibitions—the Kinsey model."

In spite of so much evidence against the credibility of his studies, the Kinsey Institute reprinted both of Kinsey's books in 1998, much to the distress of one of the child victims of the infamous Table 34.

Esther, who was four years old at the time of her father's abuse, remembers having to meet with Alfred Kinsey and talk about these experiences. She also recalls her father looking at his watch while abusing her and then filling out a questionnaire and sending it to Kinsey. The fact that these erroneous figures were published again in 1998 infuriated her.

"They used me," she said. "And they used those children and that's a terrible way to feel, that you've been used for a lie, and they perpetuated it so that it would happen again..."

And again, and again, as the lie is now taught to children as young as five years old in sex-ed programs across the nation.

The Kinsey Institute is well aware of what could happen if the public is ever allowed access to its archives, and for this reason, they refuse to let anyone see their records. This includes the authorities.

"If the FBI were to come and demand to see our histories," Kinsey photographer Clarence Tripp once said to biographer Gawthorne-Hardy, "I would destroy them first."

Conclusion

The legacy of Alfred C. Kinsey's twisted life and work can be read daily in the ever-worsening moral condition of our country. Since the onset of the sexual revolution, the rates of divorce, abortion, out-of-wedlock births, sexually-transmitted diseases, and sex crimes are the highest level ever recorded in the history of this nation.

When is enough *enough*?

Unfortunately, Hollywood is about to release a film version of Kinsey's life that glorifies the bogus research of the late Indiana University zoologist. The film stars Liam Neeson as Kinsey and was written and directed by the openly-homosexual Bill Condon. According to Dr. Judith Reisman, the film continues the fifty-year-old deception of the American public by portraying Kinsey as an authentic scientist.

"The film presents Kinsey as a bi-sexual, adventurous, pioneering man who was deeply distressed by a repressive society that had narrowed his sexual options," Reisman said. "It has something in it about the skewed statistics and the child research, but these are smoothed over."

The Kinsey Institute is a staunch supporter of the film, hoping it will restore Kinsey's tarnished image and, of course, its own financial interests. These may be difficult goals to achieve, especially given the recent conclusion of the American Legislative Exchange Council—with a membership of more than 2,400 state legislators from around the country—that Kinsey's work presents evidence of "illegal and criminal acts masquerading as science." These lawmakers were commissioned to do the research "because of widespread use of 'junk' science misdirecting legislatures, courts and education," according to their report.

For this reason, the Kinsey Institute and its faithful followers in the industries that have reaped the most benefits from Kinsey's research—Hollywood and the porn industry—have embarked on a massive advertising campaign to promote the movie and make every Kinsey critic look like a "religious fanatic."

The extent of Hollywood's hypocrisy could not have been more apparent than when the "bible" of the entertainment industry, *Variety*, refused to run an ad by Dr. Reisman depicting the Nazi pedophile with whom Kinsey consorted for his child sex data. "What I find amazing is that this is the same industry that's always screaming about censorship," Reisman said. "Whatever happened to free speech."

Apparently, only Michael Moore gets that privilege in Hollywood these days.

What can we do about this?

The first thing to do is contact Myriad Pictures and insist that Hollywood stop producing films like *Kinsey* that misrepresent and hide facts that the American public has a right to know. Myriad Pictures can be contacted at 405 South Beverly Drive, 5th Floor, Beverly Hills, CA 90212. Phone: (310) 279-4000; Fax: (310) 279-4001. Their website is www.myriadpictures.com

Next, demand that American television producers play fair by airing the other side of the Kinsey story, portrayed so well in the Yorkshire documentary produced by Tim Tate, *Secret History: Kinsey Pedophiles*. Contact the major networks, local TV stations, and cable providers and ask them to air this documentary during prime time.

Alumni of Indiana University should not hesitate to write to the university president and members of the board of directors expressing their disapproval of the university's continued support of the Kinsey Institute. "These kinds of letters drive them nuts," Dr. Reisman says. "But you don't have to be an alumnus to write." Visit the Indiana University website for the names and addresses of board members: www.indiana.edu/~iuf/people/board_directors.shtml

Parents need to be vigilant about the content of their children's sex education programs. According to Dr. Reisman, "If you have accredited people teaching sex ed in the classroom, it is Kinsey-based. The only time this isn't true is if you have something that is strictly—and I mean strictly—abstinence education. Otherwise, it is Kinsey-based."

An excellent book on how to get Kinsey-based sex education out of our nation's classrooms is available for a nominal cost from STOPP International. It is entitled *Parent Power: How Parents Can Gain Control of the School Systems That Educate Their Children,* by James W. Sedlak. This book is available on-line at www.all.org/stopp/pp15.htm or can be ordered by calling (540) 659-4171.

Movie Review

NORMALIZING PROMISCUITY AND PERVERSION

by Dr. Tom Snyder, Editor of MovieGuide.com

HOLLYWOOD, Calif.—*Kinsey* is a pseudo-intellectual new movie lionizing the work of Alfred C. Kinsey, the controversial sex researcher who launched the so-called Sexual Revolution. Kinsey was a secular humanist and anti-Christian bigot who used clearly-prejudiced pseudo-scientific methods to revive a pagan, hedonistic worldview of sexual victimization and exploitation. Effectively, Kinsey's work led legally and culturally to a normalization of sexual promiscuity, adultery, and a broad spectrum of dehumanizing sexually destructive conduct.

The movie begins by showing Kinsey's father, a Methodist Sunday School teacher, speaking out against dancing and other behavior that leads to sex, including masturbation. It then shifts to a scene of the teenage Kinsey, now a Boy Scout leader, advising another teenage Boy Scout about how to avoid the temptation of masturbation. Cut to a scene of Kinsey masturbating in his own tent at night and crying afterwards because of the guilt and shame. The movie briefly shows the development Kinsey's life-long love affair with the woods and natural science.

Eventually, much to the chagrin of his prudish father who wants him to become an engineer, Kinsey becomes a staid biology teacher at Indiana University, where he is famous for his studies of the behavior and sex life of the gull wasp. He falls in love with and marries Clara McMillen, or "Mac" as Kinsey calls her, one of his students. The couple discovers they have a sexual problem, however. Kinsey decides to consult a gynecologist, who tells them that Clara has an extra tough hymen which must be surgically broken before the couple can have proper intercourse. Cut to a montage of the couple finally enjoying their sex life, with one brief shot of them having intercourse.

Kinsey is obviously upset that he and his wife, both of whom the movie presents as virgins, have had no human sex education. The students allegedly lobby for a marriage class, which perhaps Kinsey can teach. The prudish hygiene professor, Thurman Rice, who teaches human sexuality and wisely advocates abstinence before marriage, objects, and the movie makes fun of his prudish, misogynist, ill-informed remarks about sex. The new university president, Herman Wells, agrees to let Kinsey teach the marriage course, and Kinsey begins by showing the students graphic photos of penises beginning to enter female vaginas. The students are initially shocked, but they clearly enjoy Kinsey's easygoing, friendly attitude about the subject and his answers to their sexual questions.

One day, Kinsey discovers that one of his male students, Clyde Martin, needs a campus job. Kinsey hires Clyde to become a researcher, statistician and interviewer for a university research project Kinsey is beginning on human sexuality. With funding from the radical Rockefeller Foundation, the university agrees to hire a team for Kinsey to produce authoritative studies on human sexuality. According to the movie, Kinsey plans to produce a study on male sexuality, a study on female sexuality, then studies on fringe sexual practices such as homosexuality, pedophilia, incest, and bestiality.

The movie then shows brief snippets of interviews with countless men and women who talk about their sexual history, feelings, and behavior. In one comical interview, the interviewer thinks an immigrant with a thick accent is saying that his first sexual experiences were with horses, but he really meant that his first experiences were with whores. The man admits, however, that he did once have an experience with a pony.

At some point, the movie claims that Clyde has had relationships with both men and women. Kinsey and Clyde go on a trip together. Kinsey is clearly attracted to Clyde's completely unclothed body, and casting the younger male as the seducer, the film has Clyde inviting Kinsey to have homosexual sex after Kinsey reveals that he now thinks that he himself is also a bisexual. This homosexual fling nearly wrecks Kinsey's marriage with Clara, who is clearly upset when Kinsey tells her the news. Kinsey reassures her that he still greatly loves her, even though he has sexual desires toward Clyde.

Some months later, however, Clyde visits Clara alone. He starts flirting with her, but Kinsey overhears part of the conversation and enters the room. Clyde declares to both of them that he, Clyde, misses and prefers sexual relationships with women. He asks Kinsey for permission to have intercourse with his wife, Clara. Kinsey is shocked to discover that Clara admits that she's partial to that idea. Both she and Clyde point out to Kinsey that she and Clyde must go ahead with the plan, or else they all would be hypocrites. Kinsey waits nervously downstairs while the adulterous coupling occurs.

A few years later, Clyde gets married to another woman, but she is clearly uncomfortable with the frankly sexual and personal discussion among Kinsey's team of researchers. As the movie continues to reveal some of the alleged history behind Kinsey's research, viewers learn that one of the other married researchers, Paul Gebhard, is having an affair with Clyde's wife. Kinsey's institute has filmed private sex movies between Kinsey's staff and their wives and lovers, including an encounter with Paul Gebhard and Clyde's wife. Eventually, Clyde and Paul get into a fight when Clyde's wife apparently expresses a desire to leave Clyde for Paul. An angry Kinsey orders Paul to quit the relationship and orders Clyde to patch things up with his wife. This apparently happens, but Clyde tells Kinsey in one scene that sexual relationships involve more than just biological urges.

The university eagerly arranges to "respectfully" publish Kinsey's volume on male sexuality in 1948. This causes quite a public stir because the volume recommends and claims there is widespread masturbation, adultery and use of prostitution among American males, even married ones. It also claims that many American males have bisexual and homosexual experiences.

The movie reveals Kinsey's problem of getting funding to complete his female study. In one of the movie's most controversial scenes, Kinsey and one of his young researchers interview a pan-sexual who proudly tells them of his sexual exploits with men, women, animals, and children. Like Kinsey, the man has proudly compiled statistics on his activities. The young researcher angrily marches out after the subject proudly reveals his statistics on his sexual abuse of children, but Kinsey stays to record the rest of the man's sexual history, although in the movie Kinsey has a slight distasteful look on his face.

Eventually, although Kinsey's Institute releases its female study, the movie claims that stress of the public controversy causes him to collapse at one point. In fact, there were other reasons for Kinsey's failing health. In another scene, Kinsey injures his penis by experimenting with some violent form of masturbation, but the movie fails to note that this kind of self-abuse controlled Kinsey since his youth. He had to feel sexual pain in order to feel sexual arousal. Kinsey's untimely death has been credited to *orchitis*, a painful disease often resulting from trauma to the sexual organs.

Despite his troubles, Kinsey is happy to learn from a lesbian adulterer that his female study helped her and her lesbian lover get over the guilt and shame of their affair. After this validation of the Kinsey Institute's normalization of perversion and promiscuity, the movie ends with an older Kinsey and his wife Clara walking in awe among the giant redwood trees. Kinsey informs her that they've got to go, because he's still got a lot of work to do before he dies.

Kinsey's sexually archaic, anti-Christian efforts to return to pre-civilized states of promiscuity and perversion have influenced many people, including Hugh Hefner, the anti-Christian, hedonistic founder of *Playboy* and the pornographic revolution. Their efforts have devastated our society and our children by normalizing the conduct that has given us sexually transmitted diseases (including the killer AIDS virus), rampant teenage pregnancy, graphic depictions of sex and violence in the mass media, irresponsible sexual promiscuity, and urban poverty and violence created by promiscuous fathers and mothers.

In 1950, the number of illegitimate births in America was low among whites and blacks. Now, the rates have soared to about 28 percent among white women and 68 percent among African-American women.

Consequently, the health and welfare of our society has suffered tremendously from such things as wanton divorce, the breakdown of the family, anti-Christian bigotry undermining the Christian heritage of Western Civilization, increasing attempts to redefine marriage and family, and the murder of millions of unborn children, who are the future of our Judeo-Christian civilization.

We could continue, but the history of this anti-Christian pseudo-science is too painful to recount in all its gory details.

Kinsey is well-acted and produced, if somewhat pedestrian in its narrative structure. Although the movie deals with his adultery, homosexuality, and some of the promiscuity and unethical scientific methods of his institute, it dutifully hides Kinsey's recruitment of and reliance upon pedophiles, prostitutes, and prison populations in his study of sexuality, especially male sexuality and child sexuality. It also fails to mention that Kinsey's scientific protocol included filming the sexual abuse of children, up to 24 hours at a time, timed with "a stop watch" as part of their alleged objective sexuality studies. The movie also glosses over Kinsey's materialistic, anti-Christian, pro-homosexual philosophy of the amoral, allegedly non-judgmental scientist. Apparently the writer and director, Bill Condon shares Kinsey's materialistic, anti-Christian, and pro-homosexual worldview. Interestingly, although Kinsey preaches non-judgmentalism, he angrily complains about America's "Puritan" culture. This, of course, is irrational. Finally, the movie contains graphic sexual content, references to perverse sexual practices, homosexual kissing, explicit male and female nudity, and very strong foul language.

In the final analysis, *Kinsey* is an abhorrent, paganist movie that hides the societal advances that are traced to traditional Christian values, flaunts an institutionalized sacred sex worldview, and revises biography and scientific history to promulgate a backwardly archaic, politically ignorant, social, political and sexual immoral philosophy.

Please address your comments on *Kinsey* to:

Peter Rice, President
Fox Searchlight Pictures
10201 West Pico Blvd., Bldg. 38
Los Angeles, CA 90035
Phone: (310) 369-4402
Website: www.fox.com

For more reviews from a Christian perspective,
visit www.movieguide.org

EDITOR'S NOTE

Some of the assertions made by Dr. Judith Reisman that are chronicled in this book have been called into question by the Kinsey Institute. However, Dr. Reisman and others continue to vigorously defend the validity of these assertions, providing extensive documentation to support their claims.

Congressional hearings were held in 1984 to investigate some of these matters. For more information on these hearings, visit the United States National Archives and Records Administration website at www.archives.gov.

In 1991, Dr. Reisman filed a lawsuit against the Kinsey Institute. For more information about this lawsuit, visit the following websites:

www.drjudithreisman.com/law.htm
Dr. Judith Reisman

www.indiana.edu/~kinsey
Kinsey Institute

About The Authors

Susan Brinkmann is a correspondent for *The Catholic Standard & Times* of the Archdiocese of Philadelphia. She is the author of two novels published by HarperCollins, and has written numerous children's plays and a national newsletter entitled "Divine Intervention." Susan received the Bernardin-O'Connor Award for Pro-Life Journalism in 2002 and 2003. She became a professed member of the Secular Order of Discalced Carmelites in October, 2000.

Dr. Judith Reisman is president of the Institute for Media Education and the author of several books, including: *Kinsey, Sex and Fraud* (Reisman, et al., 1990) *Soft Porn Plays Hardball* (1991), *Partner Solicitation Language as a Reflection of Male Sexual Orientation* (with Johnson, 1995), and *Kinsey: Crimes & Consequences* (1998, 2000). She is also the author of the U.S. Department of Justice's study, *Images of Children, Crime and Violence in Playboy, Penthouse, and Hustler* (1989). Dr. Reisman has served as a consultant to the U.S. Departments of Justice, Education, and Health and Human Services, and is listed in several "Who's Who" publications: *Who's Who in Science & Engineering, International Who's Who in Sexology, International Who's Who in Education, Who's Who of American Women, and The World's Who's Who of Women.*

ACKNOWLEDGMENTS

Many thanks to:

- **Dr. Judith Reisman**, for her tireless efforts over the past two decades for her research into the work of Alfred Kinsey.

- **Michelle Johnson**, editor of the *Catholic Standard and Times*, and her dedicated staff for their assistance in making this book a reality.

- **Dr. Ted Baehr**, chairman of the Christian Film & Television Commission and publisher of MovieGuide.com, for his help with the project.

- **Kinsey** *(no relation)* **Caruth** for his art direction.

Books by Dr. Judith Reisman

Kinsey, Crimes, and Consequences. Crestwood, KY: The Institute for Media Education, 1998, 2000.

Soft Porn Plays Hardball. Lafayette: LA: Huntington House, 1991.

Kinsey, Sex and Fraud. Lafayette LA: Huntington House, 1990.

Images of Children, Crime & Violence in Playboy, Penthouse, *and* Hustler. Washington, DC: United States Department of Justice, 1986, 1989, 1990. Grant No. 84-JN-AX-K007

* * *

To place an order for any of the books listed above, write to:
Dr. Judith Reisman
c/o The California Protective Parents Association
PO Box 15284
Sacramento, CA 95851-0284

Or send a fax: 1-309-412-4193

Or an email: jareisman@surewest.net

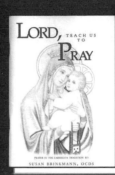

KinseyOutreach.com is a project of Catholic Outreach.

Catholic Outreach

For a list of resources to help you counteract the harmful work of Alfred Kinsey, visit www.CatholicOutreach.com